Families and

by
Heather Butler
Illustrated by Simon Smith

Hello there!

I'm Heather and I'm really glad you've joined us on this Livewires adventure. I'm feeling rather cross with Boot—I'm sure he's got something up his sleeve and he won't tell me what it is! He says I'll have to wait and see like everyone else. In which case I'll hand over to Little Ben 'cos I know he's itching to write to you...

Oh, and don't forget to fill in the special things you're doing on the diary pages—I've put down a few thoughts to start you off, but there's plenty of room to add your own feelings...

See ya!

Text copyright © Heather Butler 1996

Illustrations copyright © Simon Smith 1996

The author asserts the moral right to be identified as the author of this work

Published by
The Bible Reading Fellowship
Peter's Way, Sandy Lane West
Oxford OX4 5HG
ISBN 0 7459 3296 7
Albatross Books Pty Ltd
PO Box 320, Sutherland
NSW 2232, Australia
ISBN 0 7324 1553 5

First edition 1996

10 9 8 7 6 5 4 3 2 1 0

All rights reserved

Acknowledgments
Unless otherwise stated, scripture quotations are taken from the Good News Bible published by The Bible Societies/HarperCollins Publishers Ltd UK © American Bible Society, 1966, 1971, 1976, 1992

A catalogue record for this book is available from the British Library

Printed and bound in Malta by Interprint Limited

**An imprint of
The Bible Reading
Fellowship**

Hi there!

If you haven't met us before, welcome to Annie-log's bedroom. That's Annie-log sitting with Boot (he's her computer). Boot's very quiet at the moment, but when Annie-log types a Bible verse on his keyboard he starts making an amazing whirring sound. Then we all get whooshed into his disc drive and into the most amazing Bible adventures. Tychi—that's Boot's mouse—has to hold on really tightly when that happens.

Annie-log's got a younger sister called Data. That's her on the bottom bunk. Half the time we wonder if she's on another planet, then she comes out with something really intelligent, or finds something we've all been searching for for ages. At breakfast this morning she announced she was going to look for a loaf of bread when we go on our next adventure. Expect she'll find one too.

Digit—that's him with the shades and an enormous spider climbing over his head—and Quartz are twins. They're in the same class as Annie-log at school. Feel sorry for their teacher!

Then there's Tim. Must be time for the annual haircut soon. At least Tempo, his dog, can see clearly.

And last of all there's me, Little Ben. I'm the youngest and... whoops! I think Annie-log's keyed something into Boot.

Yes I did. Genesis—that's right at the beginning of the Bible.

Here we go. See you on the next page!

With a whirr and a whoosh the Livewires found themselves spinning through Boot's disk drive. They could no longer see Annie-log's room or feel the ground underneath them. Before they knew it their legs were being scraped by scratchy branches and they had landed in a tree. They seemed to be high above the ground. What a start to their adventure!

GENESIS 35:22

Jacob had twelve sons

Look at Boot's screen. I think this must be a family tree.

Twelve brothers. And what amazing names!

Abraham
|
Isaac
|
Esau and Jacob
|
Reuben, Simeon, Levi, Judah, Issachar, Zebulun, Joseph, Benjamin, Dan, Naphtali, Gad, Asher

Can you see whose name is right at the top? . . . .

Which do you think sounds the strangest? . . . .

```
I S S A C H A R
R I H S P O Y E
D M A H Q U I U
A E D E U L V B
G O U R F S E E
A N J D M I L N
I L A T H P A N
D N U L U B E Z
B E N J A M I N
```

The names of eleven of the brothers are on the wordsearch. Which one's missing?

. . . .

The Livewires scrambled out of the tree by helping each other. They were feeling rather cross with Boot, but he was too busy to notice. His screen is showing another Bible verse, but something has happened. Everything's written backwards! Oh no! Boot's thinking backwards. Can you work out what he's saying?

'Hello,' thought Data, 'that must be Joseph over there.' She wandered over for a chat.

Joseph told Data how it had all started—with HIM telling tales about them— and ended up with THEM throwing him down this well. He was his Dad's favourite —that was the main problem. He'd liked it at first, but later wished they'd all been treated the same.

Have you ever had something happen which seemed unfair at the time? How did you feel about it? Write or draw a picture of it on the well.

Dear God, help me always to be fair with my friends and family. Amen.

Tim had been listening to Joseph. He wasn't sure Joseph sounded a very nice person. He asked Boot what he'd done to make his brothers want to throw him down a well.

"Jacob loved Joseph more than all his other sons... He made a long robe with full sleeves for him. When his brothers saw that their father loved Joseph more than he loved them, they hated their brother so much that they would not speak to him."

GENESIS 37:3

Tim couldn't decide whether it was Joseph's fault or not. What do you think?

The brothers have left their coats on the washing line. Can you spot which two are the same? Which one do you think belongs to Joseph?

Dear God, help me not to get angry and jealous when my friends and family have things that I would like. Amen.

What are Quartz and Joseph dreaming about, Boot?

One night Joseph had a dream, and when he told his brothers about it, they hated him even more. He said, 'Listen to the dream I had. We were all in the field tying up sheaves of wheat, when my sheaf got up and stood up straight. Yours formed a circle round mine and bowed down to it.' 'Do you think you are going to be a king and rule over us?' his brothers asked. So they hated him even more because of his dreams and because of what he said about them.

Then Joseph had another dream and said to his brothers. 'I had another dream in which I saw the sun, the moon, and eleven stars bowing down to me.' He also told the dream to his father, and his father scolded him. 'What kind of a dream is that? Do you think that your mother, your brothers and I are going to come and bow down to you?' Joseph's brothers were jealous of him, but his father kept thinking about the whole matter.

GENESIS 37: 5-8 & 9-11

Joseph's not making it easy for himself. Even Quartz, who usually likes everyone, was thinking twice about him.

Data's dreaming about something, too. Her tummy's telling her it's getting near lunch time. Any ideas what she'll find to eat?

Did you find what Data was dreaming about? Because they're friends I'm sure they'll be sharing it later on. But first of all, they want to find out how Joseph was getting on with his brothers.

GENESIS 37:12-14

One day when Joseph's brothers had gone to Shechem to take care of their father's flock, Jacob said to Joseph, 'Go and see if your brothers are safe and if the flock is all right; then come back and tell me.'

Well, that seems simple enough.

But I think Joseph's brothers are planning to teach him a lesson. I've written it down in a code we learnt at school: a=26, b=25, c=24 and so on. Can you work out what they want to do?

They said to one another

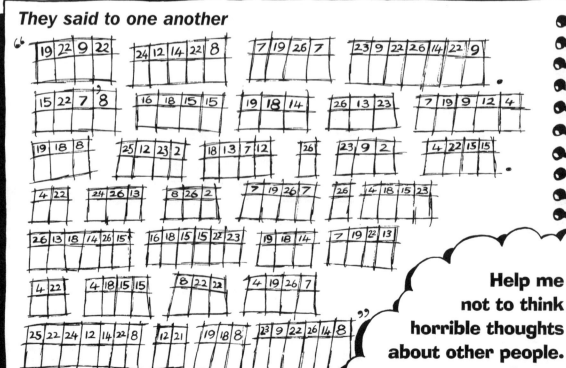

Help me not to think horrible thoughts about other people. Amen.

Annie-log was horrified when she saw what Digit found out. She quickly typed 'WHAT NEXT?' into Boot's keyboard.

> RENEUB heard them and tried to SVRE Joseph. 'Let's not LIHL him,' he said. 'Just TWROH him into this well in the ILERWNOSES, but don't RTUH him.' He said this, planning to save him and send him back to his HFRATE. When Joseph came up to his ROSTBHER, they RPIPOE FOF his LGON BRED with LFLU SSEEELV. Then they took him and HTWRE him into the ELWL, which was dry.
>
> GENESIS 37: 21-24

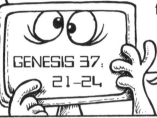

Whoops! Boot's decided to scramble up some of the words. Can you help Tychi unscramble them?

Joseph told Annie-log that he had been scared and lonely, but he soon realized that God had a plan. Joseph learnt the hard way to trust God and later he told the Livewires what happened to him after he had been thrown down the well. But that's another adventure which the Livewires had later on.

Dear God, thank you that you have a plan for my life. Help me to learn to trust you.

DIARY

SUNDAY
Who would I put in my family tree?
Who would I rather NOT have in my family tree?

MONDAY
The hardest person to get on with that I know is...

TUESDAY
When was I last treated unfairly? What did I do?

WEDNESDAY
Have I been extra nice to anyone today?

THURSDAY
Wonder what I'll dream tonight?

FRIDAY
What's God's plan for my life? I'll have to trust him about...

SATURDAY
Data's pinwheel surprise: take a slice of bread and spread it with your favourite topping. Cut off crusts, roll piece of bread round like a Swiss roll, stick cock-tail sticks through it and cut into slices. Keep an eye on Tempo!

The Livewires were thinking about Data's pinwheel surprises—they didn't spot that Boot was ready to move on. Suddenly they realized that the whirring noise had started up again and felt themselves whisked away...

The Livewires left the hot desert. They could feel the coolness you find inside a building on a hot day and, looking around, realized they were in someone's kitchen. As the dust settled they saw there was someone standing over the other side of the room. Annie-log asked Boot where they were. He started telling them something, but the Livewires couldn't make sense of what he was saying? Can you help them sort it out?

> Naomi without was or sons alone, left all husband.

RUTH 1:5

Really, Boot could be so annoying sometimes! So the lady's name was Naomi.

Naomi told them how there had been a famine in Bethlehem where she was living, so she'd gone with her husband and two sons to the foreign country of Moab to find food. They'd stayed there a long time; her sons had married Moabite girls and settled down. After some years, first Naomi's husband then her two sons died.

Joseph thought there was a plan to everything that happened to him. Do you think so too?

Oh, yes, I do. But I had to learn to trust in God. It wasn't always easy, I can tell you.

Can you think of times when you've had to trust that things would come out right, even when they seem very hard?

Help me to trust your plan even when hard things happen. Amen.

Tim wondered how Naomi had managed on her own in Moab. She told him about her son's wives, who were called Orpah and Ruth. They'd been great. One of them even came back to Bethlehem with her when she returned home. Then Boot started flickering and everyone looked at his screen. Naomi was very impressed because 'that cube thing on wheels' was showing the promise Ruth made to her in Moab.

RUTH 1:16

Let me go with you. Your people will be my people and your God will be my God.

He has a name, actually. He's called Boot and he's a computer.

Sorry, only I've never met anything like him before. Anyway, my friends couldn't believe it was me when I arrived back in Bethlehem. It was lovely to see them all again. I told them all about the sad times I'd been through.

Help me to stick by my friends when they're having a rough time. Amen.

Write down or draw anyone you know who's finding life difficult at the moment. Can you think how you can help make their life happier?

Naomi was telling Annie-log and Data about how very poor she and Ruth had been when they first came back to Bethlehem. At harvest time, Ruth went to a field and walked behind the harvesters picking up the corn that hadn't been collected. She didn't know who the field belonged to until the owner turned up. He told her his name was Boaz.

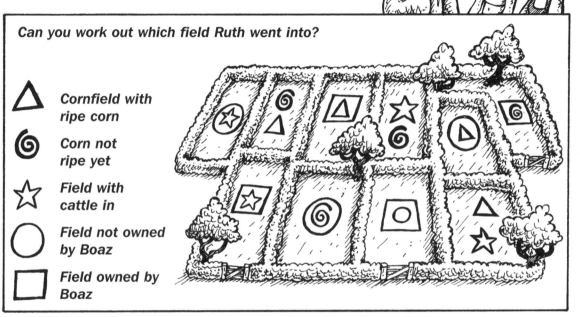

Can you work out which field Ruth went into?

△ Cornfield with ripe corn
⊚ Corn not ripe yet
☆ Field with cattle in
○ Field not owned by Boaz
▢ Field owned by Boaz

Naomi's eyes shone as she told the Livewires about Boaz. Boot knew the story and, leaning round, typed into his keyboard.

RUTH 2:20

The Lord always keeps his promises. That man is a close relative of ours, one of those responsible rof taking race fo su.

Boot, do behave! You should be explaining that by Jewish law, if possible, a widow would marry her husband's closest relative. So Boaz would be one of the people who should look after Naomi and Ruth if they didn't have husbands.

Can you work out how Boot should have finished his sentence? The Livewires couldn't imagine why he was behaving so strangely.

Quartz is the first to realize what's happened to Boot. His screen reads 'INS'T UHRT WDLONRFEU'. 'I think he's in love,' she says.

It was very important for Ruth to find another husband who would care for her, and for me, when we got older.

Our Mum works.

It was so different for us. We'd come back to Bethlehem with nothing. When Ruth said she'd met Boaz, I realized this was one of my close relatives who could look after us both.

Naomi told Ruth to put on her best dress and go to Boaz in the hope he'd fall in love with her. He did as well!

Soppy yuk!

There was one little problem though: there was another relative closer to Ruth than Boaz. So maybe it wasn't going to work out after all.

Think of a close relative and a distant relative. Pray for them now and thank God for the people who care for you.

So Boot's in love, Ruth's in love and Boaz is going to have to do something about this closer relative if he wants to marry Ruth. What a carry on! Boaz got a move on. He found the closer relative and they went to the town leaders. The other man didn't want to marry Ruth so he gave Boaz his sandal which, in those days, was the custom if you could, but didn't want to marry someone. Data wanted to know what Ruth was doing while all this was going on.

Find these words in the wordsearch. Can you remember anything about them from Naomi's story?

sandal,
Naomi,
Ruth,
Boaz,
plan,
promise,
death,
love,
Orpah

```
W O N A L P
Z R H I O R
A P T M V O
O A A O E M
B H E A K I
L A D N A S
R U T H L E
```

Write a prayer which uses three of the words in the search.

DIARY

SUNDAY
The worst experience of my life was...

MONDAY
My best friends are...

TUESDAY
Did you know that the word 'corn' is the name for the seeds of plants AND the plants themselves; like wheat, oats, barley or maize?

WEDNESDAY
The person who cares for ME is...

THURSDAY
The person I most care about is...

FRIDAY
Next time I visit a relative will they say 'haven't you grown' like they usually do!?

SATURDAY
acorn, cornfield, corner, cornet. How many more words with the word corn in can you think of?

Let's move on, Boot, and this time try not to fall in love. Promise!

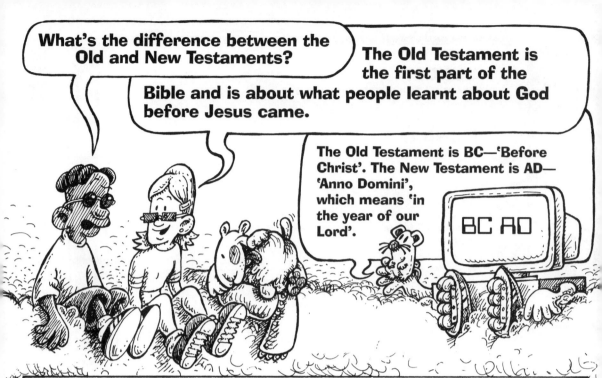

The New Testament is the second part of the Bible and is all about Jesus.

Which of these are AD and which are BC?

Titanic ship sinking BC/AD

Joseph being sold by his brothers BC/AD

Jesus healing a blind man BC/AD

The FA cup BC/AD

Boaz marrying Ruth (sorry Boot) BC/AD

Can you work out how many years there are between these dates? (clue: BC counts down to Jesus' birth; AD counts up from Jesus' birth.)

12BC to AD45

57BC to AD56

AD1978 to AD1998

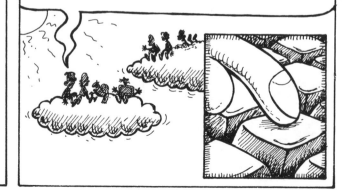

The Livewire kids came to earth with a bump, narrowly missing a nearby tree and nearly landing on a lady. They introduced themselves to her and apologized for their sudden arrival. 'We never quite know where we'll end up,' Digit sighed. The lady laughed and said she was Mary the mother of Jesus. Quartz was about to say she looked different from the picture she had of her in her Bible when Boot bleeped.

Quartz wanted to know something. If she had a dream, was it God talking to her? Mary smiled and said that God used lots of ways to speak to us. She told them how God had sent an angel to tell her about Jesus. Can you work out some of the ways God uses to talk to us?

gnidaer eht elbiB

gniyarp

woh uoy leef tuoba gnihtemos

peed edisni

enoemos gniklat ot uoy

Dear God, thank you that we can talk to you and that you answer our prayers. Amen.

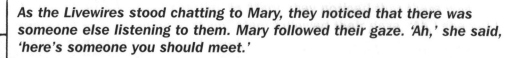

As the Livewires stood chatting to Mary, they noticed that there was someone else listening to them. Mary followed their gaze. 'Ah,' she said, 'here's someone you should meet.'

"Are we in AD?"

"I think so—let's see who Mary wants to introduce us to."

The man told them his name was Simeon and that he was a prophet. Data had to tell Little Ben what a prophet was. She had the sort of brain that was good at remembering what words meant.

"He or she speaks God's words for Him."

"Coo! So when has Simeon spoken God's words?"

"With my own eyes I have seen your salvation, which you have prepared in the presence of all peoples: A light to reveal God's will to the Gentiles and to bring glory to your people Israel."

LUKE 2: 30-32

"Mary and Joseph brought Jesus to me at the temple. I knew straight away he was God's son and had been sent by God."

"Coo! Can you tell Tempo how to go through a maze?"

"I could do, but that wouldn't be a prophecy. That would be ME speaking, not God."

Can you help Tempo find his bone? When you reach the bone write BC on it if you think the Livewires are in BC time or AD if you think they are in AD time.

Digit liked the maze puzzle and it got him thinking about a code he'd learnt at school. He whispered something in Boot's ear... Boot smiled.

Can you work out Digit's code?
Here's a clue: d=9, e=10, f=11 etc.

LUKE 2:40

The Livewires put their heads together to work out the code—they were so busy they didn't notice a boy standing watching them until he spoke...

Who are you?

I live round here

Do you know anything about Jesus? Everyone else round here seems to.

Oh yes, I knew him when he lived in Nazareth.

What was he like?

The boy told them some details. Which one's wrong?
- he was the oldest in his family
- he ate bread
- he learnt to be a carpenter
- he put up with Roman soldiers
- he watched television
- he learnt about the Jewish faith
- he had a cousin called John
- he read the scriptures

Thank you Jesus that you know what it's like to be a child. Thank you that you understand when it's hard. Amen.

The boy told the Livewires that he was on his way home from city of Jerusalem. As the Livewires chatted to him a crowd of people started to come down the road.

The boy explained that it was Passover and loads of people had been to celebrate the festival in Jerusalem. Everyone was going home now, most of them travelling in large family groups. Tim spotted Mary pushing her way through the crowd the wrong way.

I've lost Jesus! I've got to find him.

Tempo and I'll come and help you look.

They went back to Jerusalem and searched all over the place. They ended up in the temple before they found Jesus.

LUKE 2:49

Didn't you know that I had to be in my Father's house?

Jesus was talking with the Jewish teachers, listening to them and asking questions. Everyone who heard him was amazed at his intelligent answers. After all, he was only twelve years old! He already seemed to know where he fitted into God's family and what God's plan was for him.

Think about the way you might fit into God's family. What plans do you think God might have for you? You might like to write your feelings in the prayer cloud and talk to God about them.

John told them about the time when he and Jesus were grown-ups. He'd been by the River Jordan baptizing people when Jesus had asked to be baptized too. When John baptized Jesus, a voice from heaven had spoken the words on Boot's screen.

Cross out all the bbbbs and you'll find some!

bblibbbebs... gbbrebbebd... cbheabbbbtbibnbgb... bbrbubdbbenbbebss... bbebnbbbbvyb..

Can you think of any more?

God can help wash you clean inside if you ask him.

DIARY

SUNDAY
Can you make up a sentence beginning with the letters BCAD? (For example: All Camels Become Dragons.)

MONDAY
In what ways has God spoken to me today?

TUESDAY
How can I tell my friends I like them without words?

WEDNESDAY
How many times have I washed my hands today?

THURSDAY
Things I want to learn about are...

FRIDAY
Everyone was a child once, even my teacher. Wonder if he/she ever got told off by their teacher?

SATURDAY
Which of these places did Jesus NOT go to as a child? Egypt, Bethlehem, Nazareth, River Jordan, Sea of Galilee, London, Jerusalem.

Boot began making his whirring sound and the children grabbed each other as they knew this meant they were about to be whisked into the disc drive. In the confusion, Data forgot about her loaf of bread and Tempo didn't have time to pick his bone up. He was NOT a happy dog, so to keep him quiet Boot promised to land somewhere especially for him.

Boot took the Livewires into the countryside. Tempo became very excited. He'd smelt something interesting. Tim was beginning to wish he'd brought his lead when a man came towards them. He was carrying a large box which he put down. Tempo rushed over to say 'hello' and before long they were all talking. The man said he was a travelling storyteller. 'Tell us a story!' the Livewires begged.

He said he'd tell them three stories about things that were lost. As the children sat down on the grass, Data began to think of all the things SHE'D lost. Sort them out for her and add two things you've lost in the past. Put the most important thing at the top of the list.

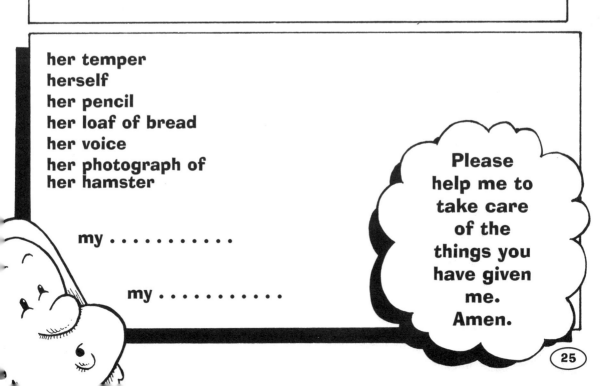

her temper
herself
her pencil
her loaf of bread
her voice
her photograph of
her hamster

my . . . .

my . . . .

Please help me to take care of the things you have given me.
Amen.

The storyteller smiled as Quartz asked him the question. 'Well done for thinking hard,' he said. 'Jesus wants to be your friend and look after you like the shepherd did. When you don't bother with him, you're like the sheep who wandered off. I reckon that sheep thought it was really cool to run away. Then the thought of wild animals came to him, and it started to get dark and I expect he was very frightened. We can try to run away from God sometimes.'

The Livewire kids thought about how they might behave like the sheep did. Can you work their ideas out from the mirror writing below?

raews
seil llet
laets
morf sgniht
sdneirf ruo
sgurd yrt

Dear God, sometimes it's hard, but please help me to stay close to you, my Good Shepherd. Amen.

I tell you, the angels of God rejoice over one sinner who repents

LUKE 15:10

Boot was enjoying himself, following the storyteller's tale, but Little Ben was puzzled. 'What does 'repent' mean?' he asked. 'It means being sorry for what you've done, and turning back to God,' the storyteller told him. 'We'd be like that if the Good Shepherd came to find us, wouldn't we?' Little Ben said. Their friend nodded. Then he told them another parable about a woman who had ten silver coins and lost one of them.

'Each coin, like each of you, was very precious. So she had to find the one which was lost. She lit a lamp, swept her house and searched. The Bible doesn't say where she found the coin, but she was so pleased when she did that she invited her friends round to celebrate, just like the angels celebrate each time someone who's done wrong says sorry and turns back to God.'

Can you reach the coin in the middle of this maze?

START

Have you ever lost anything which was important to you? How did you feel about it?

Here's my last story. It's about a boy who lived on a farm with his dad and his brother.

Tempo woofed quietly and sat up at the mention of the farm. There might be some animals to sniff out! But the story started with the boy asking his father for money—money that would normally have been given to him when his dad died and the farm was shared between him and his brother. He then left home and spent it all. It didn't last very long and after it was gone his so called 'friends' left him. He ended up getting a job feeding pigs...

PIGS!

Tempo, settle down!

Sheep aren't as clever as people and coins don't have brains, but the boy did and he chose to leave home, didn't he? So does that mean we can deliberately choose to go away from God?

The storyteller sighed. 'Yes, and many people do. It makes God so sad, like the father was in the story. Every day he looked for his son, waiting and hoping he'd come home again.'

The Livewires sat very quietly for a few minutes just thinking about what the storyteller had said. What would your thoughts be if you were with them?

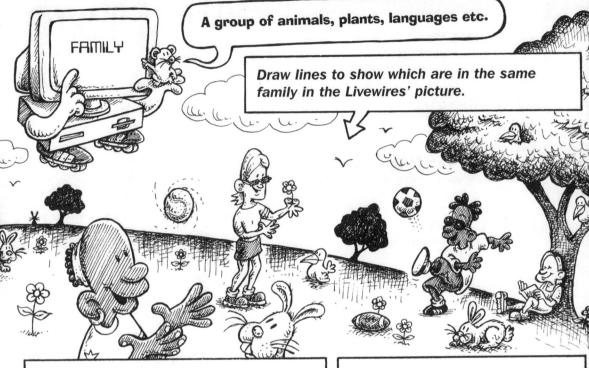

Forty winks later, Boot was full of energy and raring to go. His screen suddenly started flashing...

A group of animals, plants, languages etc.

Draw lines to show which are in the same family in the Livewires' picture.

Who are the members of your family?
Do you always get on with them?
What do you like doing together?

Boot's found two places in the Bible about families. If you have a Bible, try looking them up. Don't forget to use the index if you get stuck. The first number is the chapter and the number after the ':' is the verse.

Dear God, sometimes it's hard and sometimes it's easy being in a family. Thank you that Jesus knows what it's like. Amen.

When God designed people he wanted them to be together, to live as families.

Which of these things can you do when you're with YOUR family? Tick the boxes.

- ☐ relax
- ☐ say what you like
- ☐ learn what living is all about
- ☐ watch TV together
- ☐ be rude to each other
- ☐ steal
- ☐ enjoy being with each other

Is there anything else you'd add?

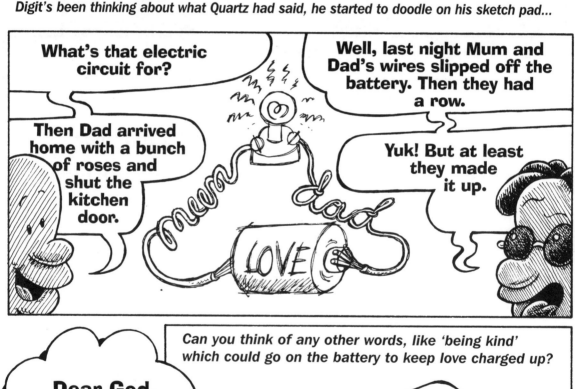

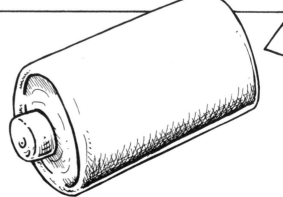

Your parents want the very best for you; that's why they tell you to do things.

Jesus loved being with children—he valued them and spent time talking to them.

Let the children come to me and do not stop them.

MARK 10:14

Quartz suddenly remembered the special 'family' day their church was having. Everyone, whatever their age, had been invited and there were going to be loads of things to do. Most people were going in fancy dress and Digit wanted to have his face painted. There were going to be competitions and craft things and lots of lovely food.

Draw a picture of something YOU would want to do if your church held a special 'family day'.

Church is like a family. What does YOUR church do to make you feel part of it?

Children will always be an important part of God's family. Never forget that—especially when you're a grown-up!

What sort of people are in God's family?

ldo   das   aft   phpya   ygonu   ihcr
dtsdloer   nkisny   lrcdhine

When you've unscrambled the words, perhaps you could think of some more and show the puzzle to a grown-up.

DIARY

SUNDAY
Do I know anyone with a name which comes from the Bible? Is their name from the Old Testament or the New? Or both!

MONDAY
Wonder if I'll be taller than my mum when I grow up?

TUESDAY
Does 'forget about it' mean the same as saying 'that's all right' when someone says 'sorry'?

WEDNESDAY
Our next family outing is going to be...

THURSDAY
Must get some new batteries for my...

FRIDAY
How do I feel when my dad calls me by my nickname?

SATURDAY
Do the older people at church really like having me as part of their family? Do I like having THEM as part of the church family?

The Livewires took a deep breath as Boot began making the familiar whirring sound. Tim grabbed Tempo and Little Ben caught Tychi as she flew past him. Time to be moving on again. But where to this time?

The Livewires are worried about Boot. He crash-landed rather heavily and scraped his elbow and he doesn't seem to know where they are. Now he's making odd noises. Tychi's trying to sort him out.

Data's right—that's Tempo's bone she's holding! Can you sort out what belongs to who?

Some things that belong to people can easily be replaced. Others can't. Tick the right boxes below.

	can	not sure	can't
Grandma			
favourite teddy			
pencil			
Tempo			
chair			
flower			

Dear God, thank you for all the people and things you've given me. Help me always to look after them properly. Amen.

Can you NEARLY belong to something without COMPLETELY belonging? How can you encourage someone who wants to join a group? Write down your thoughts here, or draw a picture.

"The world   belong   all who live in it are HIS"

"Boot's written 'HIS' in capital letters. I think it's because HIS means God's."

Quartz is right - everything in the world belongs to God. And Christians are his family on earth. But there's more to it than that. God made everyone, even if they ignore him or even think he doesn't exist. Everyone belongs to God and he wants them to love him and join his family on earth. How can you encourage someone to become part of God's family?

Why not tell God about someone who doesn't know him now?
How do you think God feels about that person?

Boot got to his feet, his screen seemed to be brighter. The Livewires were pleased to see that he was feeling better. They're going to take more care of him next time he starts whirring at them.

The world and all that is in it belong to the Lord.

PSALM 24:1

Everyone agreed that the world is a beautiful place. God lets us use it, but do we always look after it as we should?

How can we take more care? Write down your ideas...

Dear God, we're sorry that we spoil your world by the things we do to it and each other. Help us to take more care by...

Perhaps you could add your own words to finish the prayer.

Boot was feeling completely better. He wrote the Bible verse out in fancy writing. Colour it in and think about the things you've learnt over the last few days. You might like to put yourself in the picture.

The World and all that is in it belong to the LORD. The earth and all who live in it are his.

Dear God, thank you for everything you have given us. Amen.

DIARY

SUNDAY
I like my bedroom because...

MONDAY
The best group I belong to is...

TUESDAY
The group I'd like to belong to is...

WEDNESDAY
Here's a picture of some people at our church...

THURSDAY
Where's my nearest recycling bin?

FRIDAY
My newest friend is...

SATURDAY
What's yellow and goes at 100 kilometres an hour?

Answer: A train driver's egg sandwich

Data's loaf of bread could make some nice sandwiches. She suddenly realized she was getting hungry. But there wasn't time to do anything about it because Boot had other ideas!

Once again Boot whisked the Livewires away. They took great care of him when they landed. Data was thinking about when she was grown up.

"The church family will always be there."

"And we'll probably start families of our own one day, then we'll be mums and dads."

They stopped talking as a lady came up to the door of the house. She smiled at them and Annie-log smiled back. The lady introduced herself. 'I'm Martha,' she said. 'Are you someone who knew Jesus when he lived on earth?' Little Ben asked. 'Oh, yes. He was part of our family' she said. 'When he left his own family to travel round the country, he often came to stay with us. This house was like a second home for him.'

Martha's house was at Bethany.

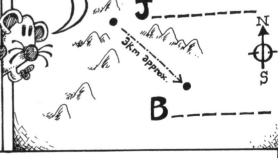

Can you find Bethany on the map?

Martha told the Livewires she shared the house with her sister, Mary, and brother, Lazarus. They loved having Jesus to stay with them. Mary used to listen and talk with him for hours and Martha used to get cross, wanting help with all the jobs that needed doing around the house.

Jesus used to point out I was fussing.

'Martha! You are worried and troubled...Mary has chosen the right thing, and it will not be taken away from her.'

Jesus knew how important it was to spend time with friends and family.

LUKE 10:41-42

Digit remembered his battery doodle. He pulled it out of his pocket and wrote 'talking' and 'spending time' on the battery.

Dear God, if I'm so busy that I don't spend enough time with my family, please show me. Amen.

When do you spend time with your family and what do you do?

Martha told them about Jesus. Digit had never heard about the time when Lazarus had become very ill. They'd sent a message to Jesus hoping he'd come and heal him. But Jesus didn't come at once, and when Lazarus died they took his body to a burial cave. Then Jesus turned up.

I am the resurrection and the life. Those who believe in me will live, even though they die.

JOHN 11:25

Resurrection means bringing something back to life

Martha was upset that Jesus hadn't been there to heal her brother, but she still wanted to trust him.

I knew that he was the son of God who was living in the world.

Dear Lord Jesus, help me to believe in you like Martha did. Amen.

The Livewires sat quietly and thought about what Martha had said. If you were Martha how would you have felt when Jesus didn't do what you expected him to? How would you have felt when it turned out all right in the end? How does this show why we should trust God?

Martha went on, 'Jesus was so sad, he cried as well. He was human like everyone else. Some people said he was upset because he'd loved Lazarus so much, others laughed and said that if he could heal blind people, why couldn't he have helped his friend?'

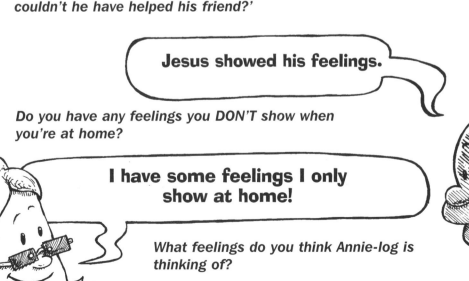

'So what did Jesus do?' Digit asked. Martha continued her story. 'He went off to the burial cave where Lazarus's body was,' she said.

Jesus told Lazarus to come out. He'd been dead for four days and everyone watching couldn't believe it. But out my brother came, wrapped up in grave clothes and with a cloth wound round his face! You see, Jesus proved to us that he had power over life and death.

'so that you would believe'

JOHN 11:15

'Yes, that's right. Jesus promised that all who believe in Him will never die. He wasn't talking about your body. That'll die, but the part of you that feels emotions and thinks—that's your spirit—if you trust Jesus, won't die when your body does; it'll go to be with God in heaven for ever.

Boot liked the sound of that so much he's done some more fancy writing for you to colour in.

"all those who believe in me will never die"

JOHN 11:26

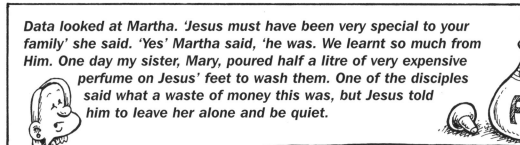

Data looked at Martha. 'Jesus must have been very special to your family' she said. 'Yes' Martha said, 'he was. We learnt so much from Him. One day my sister, Mary, poured half a litre of very expensive perfume on Jesus' feet to wash them. One of the disciples said what a waste of money this was, but Jesus told him to leave her alone and be quiet.

The sweet smell of the perfume filled the whole house.

Mary was giving Jesus a gift that cost a lot of money and Jesus accepted it.

JOHN 12:3

Often families give each other expensive presents which don't cost ANY money. Can you work out which is the most 'expensive' thing here? There is no right or wrong answer!

a new car

Dad playing a game with you instead of going to sleep in front of the TV

your favourite teddy

new clothes

a trip to the cinema with mum

a family holiday

a new computer

a hug

Dear Lord Jesus, help me find ways I can give things to my family and my friends. Amen.

SUNDAY
Here's a picture of me and my family when I've grown up...

MONDAY
How long have I spent talking with my family today?

TUESDAY
The feelings that make me cry are...

WEDNESDAY
I trust Jesus because...

THURSDAY
If I were to design a birthday cake for my best friend, this is what it would look like...

FRIDAY
Biscuit recipe. Mix 150g butter, 100g sugar then add 2 egg yolks, 225g plain flour and 20ml water. Make little balls and put on to grease proof paper, cooking 6 at a time in a microwave oven at full power for 2–2 1/2 minutes.

SATURDAY
Things I do for my family are...

Quartz asked Boot if he knew of any other families in the New Testament.

ACTS 18:2

As Boot flashed the Bible verse onto his screen the Livewires were once more whisked away in a cloud of dust. Hang on tight! You'll find them on the next page...

As the dust started to settle the Livewires could see a map spread out beneath them.

Boot pulled a fact file into his screen...

Where do you think Boot is going to land? Can you find where you think it will be on the map?

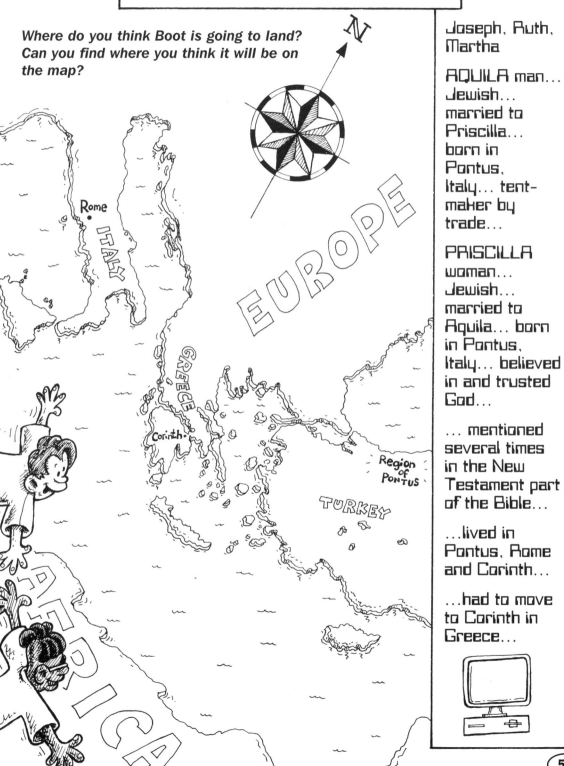

Joseph, Ruth, Martha

AQUILA man... Jewish... married to Priscilla... born in Pontus, Italy... tent-maker by trade...

PRISCILLA woman... Jewish... married to Aquila... born in Pontus, Italy... believed in and trusted God...

... mentioned several times in the New Testament part of the Bible...

...lived in Pontus, Rome and Corinth...

...had to move to Corinth in Greece...

The Livewires landed with a bump in the town of Corinth, right outside Aquila and Priscilla's house. They knocked on the door and were invited in. A meal was laid with enough places for everyone and soon they were tucking in to Priscilla's wonderful cooking, and some of Data's loaf of bread.

It didn't take long before they'd discovered that Aquila and Priscilla had been born in Pontus, Italy, but had had to leave because the Roman Emperor Claudius had ordered all Jewish people to leave Rome.

They'd been refugees when they arrived in Corinth. It had been hard leaving friends behind, but the church family in Corinth helped them settle in a new place. They were tent-makers and soon began working hard. Later, they saw how God's plan was clever because they were just where He needed them to help other people.

A refugee is someone who has lost their home and had to move away from their home town or country.

Which of these sentences is right?

Aquila was a woman.

Priscilla was not Jewish.

Aquila and Priscilla went to Italy.

They lived before Jesus was born.

They made tents.

Roman Emperors were always kind and thoughtful.

Dear God, if I go somewhere new, please help me to make friends quickly. Help me too to make friends with people who are new to the place where I live. Amen.

Can you think of people in the news who have become refugees? Why did this happen to them? How do you think they feel? Perhaps you can think of ways you could help them.

A friend of ours called Paul used to travel round the country telling people about Jesus. He used to stay with us when he was in Corinth.

Priscilla told the Livewires how tired Paul was after preaching in the temple, or after a long journey. God had given them their home, so they used it to help other Christians. They'd even used it to have church services in. It was something they could do for God. If each person did what they could, it was like a body with all the parts working together.

What do each of the parts of Data's body do?

Nice bread. My body needs feeding or it won't grow.

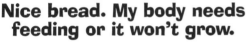

That reminded Boot of something. He reached round to type on his keyboard...

If the whole body were just an eye, how could it hear?

Tychi thought that was very funny. She rolled around on the floor, holding her sides with her paws. You could draw a picture of the body just being an eye... or just an ear... or just a mouth... Use your imagination.

HA HA HA

Dear God, thank you for our bodies. Thank you for making us so special. Amen.

1 CORINTHIANS 12:17

Aquila and Priscilla had travelled with Paul on one of his missionary journeys. It had helped them to know what difficulties he faced. Not everyone wanted to hear about Jesus, and Paul was sometimes beaten up or thrown out of the town for talking about him.

Tychi knew what Paul had said about Aquila and Pricilla so she whispered in Boot's ear...

They risked their lives for me. I am grateful to them.

ROMANS 16:4

We were so glad our friends in Corinth were praying for us. I know it helped us cope with the rough times we had.

I'm not old enough to do some things, but I CAN pray for the people who do do them.

That's being part of a body!

God's Church is like a body, and his people are his Church.

Some people are like eyes in the Church—they look out for other people. Some are like ears—they listen to others. Some are like hands—they help others.

You might like to write a prayer to God in this bubble about the part of God's Church that you would like to be...

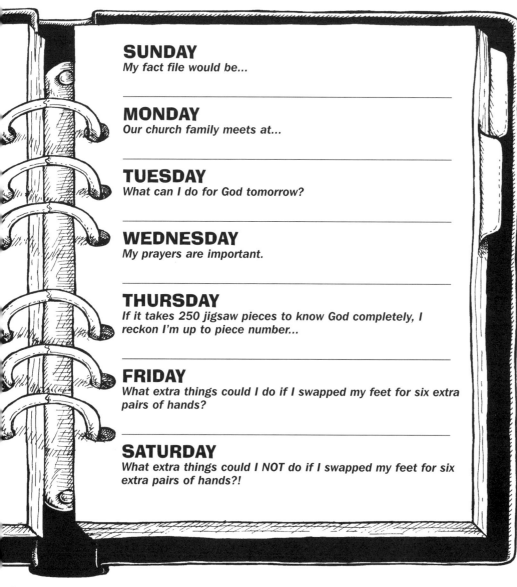

DIARY

SUNDAY
My fact file would be...

MONDAY
Our church family meets at...

TUESDAY
What can I do for God tomorrow?

WEDNESDAY
My prayers are important.

THURSDAY
If it takes 250 jigsaw pieces to know God completely, I reckon I'm up to piece number...

FRIDAY
What extra things could I do if I swapped my feet for six extra pairs of hands?

SATURDAY
What extra things could I NOT do if I swapped my feet for six extra pairs of hands?!

Data's shared her loaf of bread with the others at Priscilla and Aquila's. She's asked Boot if they can go somewhere so she can make some more. Ever ready to oblige, Boot starts to whirr...

As the Livewires landed they bumped into an old friend. Can you remember who she is?

Hello again! I want to make some bread. Will you help me?

You'd better come in to my kitchen where I've got flour and yeast.

Here are some of the things Tempo sniffed in the food store in Martha's kitchen. Can you see what was there?

Dear God, thank you for our food. Thank you especially for...

Data looked inside the bag of corn. Something needed to be done to it before she could use it to make any bread. 'This is going to take a long time,' she sighed.

How many of the things Tempo found in Martha's store cupboard would you find in your cupboard at home? What things in your cupboard wouldn't have been in Martha's?

You might like to think about those things and write a prayer about them.

Martha took the children to her corn mill. Corn was put between the two heavy stones. As the top one was moved around, the corn was ground into flour. Two people were usually needed to work it.

Martha explained that it was the women who cooked and prepared all the food.

Well, today it'll be different. Little Ben and I'll help grind the corn to make the flour for Data's bread.

Watch out for the noise!

Tim told Martha about all the gadgets his mum had in her kitchen. Martha laughed. The nearest thing she had to a fridge was a cold stone with a cloth over the food to keep the flies off. Water came from a well in the middle of the village. She had to fetch it in large jars which she carried on her head. The well was by the village press which everyone used to squeeze oil out of olives. While Tim and Little Ben worked, Digit and Quartz helped make a fire. This would heat the oven to cook Data's bread when it was ready.

Put a tick in the right box.

	today we have:	in the Bible people had:
corn	❏	❏
bread	❏	❏
olives	❏	❏
microwaves	❏	❏
marrow	❏	❏
dishwashers	❏	❏
water	❏	❏
crisps	❏	❏
fish fingers	❏	❏

Boot rubbed his tummy as he watched the Livewires making the bread.

Thank you, God, for what keeps me going; things like disk drives, electricity, microchips, leads, wires, plugs and computer games. Amen.

Little Ben had been thinking as he ground the corn. 'What makes the bread rise?' he asked.

"A woman takes some yeast and mixes it with flour until the whole batch of dough rises."

"Boot's right—and that's how Jesus used to describe God's kingdom in the world—like yeast working its way through dough to make it light and tasty."

LUKE 13:20-21

Martha went on to explain that during the festival of Passover, the Jewish people wouldn't put yeast in the bread to make it rise. This kind of bread was called unleavened bread. 'If it HAD been Passover, you could always have gone to a Roman's house and found some yeast,' she said, 'THEY didn't keep Jewish festivals.'

Little Ben wanted to know if the food the Romans ate was different to the food Martha and her friends ate. He wasn't that surprised when she said that it was. Rich Romans had four meals a day instead of two, with lots of servants to cook and prepare. They regularly ate meat, often spending up to three hours over their evening meal, eating with their fingers and reclining at low, semi-circular tables.

By the time Martha had finished talking, Data had just finished preparing the dough. She'd added the yeast to the flour and kneaded it to mix it together. Now she put it in a dish and left it to rise before cooking it.

Matthew 7:9
Matthew 7:10
Matthew 13:31 Sounds like
Numbers 11:32
Numbers 13:20

While the Livewires were waiting for the bread to rise they played a game about some of the places in the the Bible where food is mentioned. Digit pulled out his sketch pad and started to doodle the clues. Can you work out which foods are mentioned here from his clues?

Dear God, thank you for giving us enough food. Please help governments to look after everyone properly, so that people won't go hungry. Help us to understand how to share your good gifts fairly. Amen.

62

They all held their breath as Boot's driver started up. Once more they felt that whooshing feeling as they headed for the disc drive. It had been good going on an adventure, but they were all glad when they landed back again in Annie-log's bedroom. They'd learnt lots of new things, now they had to remember some of them! (And Data, of course, had her loaf of bread.) 'I think it's time to eat,' she said, and began breaking the bread and sharing it out. Tempo licked up the crumbs before settling down for a long sleep.